Copyright © 2022 LaTonya D. McElroy

All rights reserved

No part of this book may be reproduced or transmitted in any form or by any means whatsoever without the express written consent from the author.

Linda D Henderson, Editor

PAPERBACK VERSION
ISBN: 9798366298773

ELECTRONIC VERSION
ISBN-13: 9781234567890
ISBN-10: 1477123456

Cover design by: LaTonya D. McElroy
Library of Congress Control Number: 2018675309
Printed in the United States of America

This book is dedicated to my HR colleagues all over, including in SHRM, in Texas SHRM, and in my local Tri-State Chapter. You have been on the forefront of massive change, and you have carried your organizations with you, both in your heart and sometimes on your shoulders. More than anything, I am immensely grateful for my family (Arthur and children, Mom-Linda and Dad-Walter, my siblings, nephews, cousins, aunts, and church family-Mt. Pisgah). Through a period of personal change, even reinvention, we have walked a journey of faith and landed on our feet through prayer. This is what God's love looks like. The most amazing times of life are happening before our eyes. Seeing how the journey intertwines is fascinating. Thanks to everyone who is connected.

FOREWORD

I once heard Jim Rohn say "success isn't pursued, it's attracted". It was an epiphany for me when I heard this as a young leader. No longer did I feel like I needed to get up each day to chase after things, but to get up each day and work on myself to get better in my career and every area of my life. And I learned that the better we get, the more we become. So when I saw the title of LaTonya McElroy's new book called "talent attraction" I was immediately drawn in. And when she asked me to write the foreword, I was so honored. You are getting to read about several strategies that will help you better attract talent throughout this book - but it really starts with the person behind the pages. LaTonya McElroy knows talent and the power of attraction. I first met LaTonya in Paris, Texas at our annual Texas SHRM state meeting to connect, support, and serve our chapter leaders across the great state of Texas. There are moments in time that just stand out in our careers and for me, it was that meeting - that moment when LaTonya stood up to share the value of certifications. After she finished her presentation, I asked her to share her perspective on a short video clip so I could share with others. I was drawn to her leadership by her heart and energy. She just made you feel like someone you could count on at any moment. I later invited LaTonya to be a guest on my "Life in the Leadership Lane" podcast where she shared her story and perspective around HR and leadership. I was then drawn in even more with her inspiration. As I reflect, I believe her true attraction comes from her heart. LaTonya has a gift that attracts people to her. It's a gift of humility, and encouragement and passion and boldness and values and heart! I'm so glad she is sharing her wisdom and heart in this book to help others. It's who she is. In "Talent Attraction," LaTonya shares her heart too… so you will be attracted just as I was. It's the differentiator - the connection for us and with others in the workplace.

Today, LaTonya is a workforce champion because of the person she has become. She's didn't pursue it - it was something that she has been attracting for the last 20 years growing her skills to serve as a business leader in HR. I am so glad she has decided to share her gifts to help us get better so that we can attract the things we want, and more importantly attract the person and team we want to become. You will be inspired. She is truly in her lane. Open your heart and turn the page… a great journey is beginning! I can't wait to see who you become.

Foreword by Bruce W. Waller

Relocation Executive, Author, Speaker and Host - Life in the Leadership Lane podcast

TALENT ATTRACTION

*Inclusive Talent Attraction
in a World of Talent Acquisition*

by LaTonya Darneish McElroy, MBA, SPHR, SHRM-SCP/TA

TABLE OF CONTENTS

Dedication

Introduction

Chapter 1

Chapter 2

Chapter 3

Chapter 4

Chapter 5

Chapter 6

Chapter 7

Conclusion

About the Author

Works Cited:

INTRODUCTION

We have recently learned that talent can no longer be acquired.

    We can acquire exercise equipment, a car, and even a company, but talent – not so much, or not for *long*. When a business acquisition takes place, one company acquires another through purchase, a financial transaction based on what is considered a fair valuation. What is the business worth? Well, that depends on who you ask. By the same standard, what dollar value can anyone place on a person's talent? How quickly can that valuation change relatively or become obsolete? By the time an employment offer is out, there is already a higher bidder. *This* has become the world of talent acquisition, becoming as inhumane to the companies racing to keep up with escalating labor expenses as it is to the person whose talent is being 'acquired.'

    Talent attraction is a shift in focus, from acquiring talent to attracting talent. While acquisition typically scouts for the opportunistic approach – finding the best talent and sweeping them into the doors for the highest performing team – talent attraction understands the value of *being* desired.

    Unemployed for the first time in 19 years, walking through the job search process in disbelief, I wonder who ever thought this was a job seekers' market. Then, I begin to string together nearly two decades of immersive real-life Human Resources experience, and I have an epiphany: there's too much exclusive acquisition and not enough inclusive attraction. Employers are hand-picking talent, and job seekers are becoming more discerning about the real culture behind the marketing and job posting campaign.

With so many vacancies and as many complaints from competent job seekers, something is definitely missing. We almost need a match-making service for recruiting. Everybody is 'open for work' and 'hiring,' but many of the finders and seekers are not connecting to one another. Even worse, the 'found' are still 'seeking.'

Another really eye-opening reality is the 'pushing and repelling' that seems to be working against the two parties: candidates and employers. Employers are often acquiring what they think they want and not attracting or recognizing what they actually need. Think of acquisition as more hand-picking candidates based on what we believe they have to offer, rather than creating a magnetic effect that draws those who both want us and also have within them what we need.

Let's shift our workplaces from the boring laws of supply and demand to the principles of attraction. People give their *all* to what they love, and what we love becomes a part of us. That's attraction.

Disclaimer: This book is written from a Christian worldview. The ideas and beliefs are not intended to represent those of anyone besides the author and do not take away from the principles shared herein, but are used as a fundamental basis for thought, belief, and self-view.

CHAPTER 1

Talent is not acquired; it's borrowed

As employees, we *lend* our talents, and that is no small loan. Afterall, our talents are God-granted, inborn, learned, earned and sharpened by a myriad of experiences that are unique to us. These talents are what we have to offer as our contribution. And, this is why these talents cannot be acquired or bought:

Our talents need, not only our time, but our energy. For example, for a professional dancer to offer their talents, they need a performance time in which to showcase their dance talents. Otherwise with little or no performance time, we get a rushed or jumbled performance or no performance at all due to lack of time. However, if we have the talent and time, but not the energy/passion, then we are again at a stand-still. Obviously, a great example of this is a sleeping ballerina or salsa dancer dragging through their performance with sluggish moves and no enthusiasm. So, our talents need our *energy*, which is our desire, want-to, enthusiasm… our *heart*.

Can we truly be satisfied with only having a claim on people's talent and time, if we do not have their heart – their desire, want-to, or enthusiasm? Who wants an unenthusiastic employee? Acquiring talent can be much like an arranged marriage, with both families having something to gain (such as wealth, territory, business dominance, or reputation), while the perfect couple shares no attraction. In the same way, while acquiring talent may even bring benefits to both parties (performance potential, salary, and medical benefits), the real powerlifter behind the employee-employer union is *want-to* and a desire to truly accomplish great things together.

Here is why we often do not receive the full package with talent acquisition. Both our energy and time are limited resources, as employees, and many things compete for priority in our lives. While as employees, where we give our time is not always a choice, whether we fully give our *energy* remains within our control. The lever of our performance is our energy, desire, and simple 'want-to.' The more we *want* to perform our work, the better we perform. The more attracted we are to the work, the people, our team, and our organizations, the more we want to give our energy there. Sometimes we do not receive the full package when acquiring talent because we have a person without the passion/energy.

Why? Because energy is limited, and we are discretionary with our energy. We give our energy to what and whom we choose. The more performance energy we give in one place, the less we have available in others, and we have the human tendency to reserve our fullest selves for the things we are truly attracted to doing and places we really want to be. This is why someone sharing their fully engaged 'talent' is a huge sacrifice and can never be truly acquired. We can employ a person and never actually receive their greatest performance potential, although we think we have 'acquired their talent,' because we can make demands on time, even coach performance, but we can never buy their passion.

The energy level is the lever for talent. Energy controls that gateway in between. If the gateway between our talent and our performance is not fully open, then our performance is limited. This is why hiring people with high-performance history, years of experience, education, and even demonstrated knowledge and skill does not guarantee high performance on our teams.

In the Bible, the king Saul was great in stature and had an amazing lineage. He should have been a high-performing king, but he was not and was intimidated by David, a ruddy shepherd boy from the field with no special family history. David, an unassuming and certainly underestimated, fearless young man, became highly celebrated and eventually replaced Saul as king. He came from nothing, had the least perceived experience, but David had *heart*.

When an employer is looking for a new employee, they should never underestimate the importance of heart. If we only measure talent and ability, we are missing the master key.

What gets measured is what is viewed as important. When we measure something, we are acknowledging its significance. So, what questions are employers asking to help determine how much energy, enthusiasm, and heart a person is bringing to their work?

Long before we consider 'acquisition,' we should be measuring attraction.

- What excites the candidate about their work?
- What is one of the most energizing projects or assignments they have done?
- What about the company excites them most and why?
- What is the best job they have ever had and why?

Questions like these, help us understand the most important aspects of candidate-to-role attraction. Then, we consider the work, the environment, and the team this individual would be joining and determine if these areas align with what attracts the employee (based on answers to questions similar to those above). While compensation and benefits are attractive, benefits and money have their limits. Passion and heart are much more valuable.

As people, we will often enthusiastically *lend* our talents and *give* our time to causes we love, even if it means giving extra time and effort above and beyond the job description.

As employers, the objective becomes matching people with what they love and becoming a team and organization that is attractive to them. In this scenario, people are more willing to lend us their talents, plus have the energy and heart to perform at a higher level.

CHAPTER 2

Employers must transition from attracting only what they already *are* to attracting what they need.

We know that a magnet is functioning properly when it has a strong pull for anything metallic, and we know that an employer is magnetic when it is naturally and organically drawing talent, but not just any talent. Magnets attract opposing charges – what they do not have.

First, however, let's talk about the five characteristics of a magnetic employer, and then we will discuss how to attract what we need, versus only what we are.

In a world of passive talent sourcing and creative job posting, we have to ask the question, why are some companies such magnets for talent, while others find it difficult to compete? Why does one employer in a similar geographic region, same industry, and even similar size draw a large candidate pool, while another struggles to receive applications?

According to an article by Jobsoid, there are 5 innovative talent attraction strategies. These strategies are a strong employer brand, an employee referral program, accommodating to employee needs, well-crafted job descriptions, and building connections through social media recruiting (Baretto, 2021).

First, employer brand has become the focus of many recruiting plans, and for the first time consistently and nearly universally, the relationship between HR and

Marketing has been sealed with this need to create the right consumer story for applicants. The brand tells the applicant-consumer who the company is (or wants to be), what the organization values, and its mission. Barretto further shares the importance of engaging existing employees in the story-telling, sharing pieces of their work-life with the public. It is the new reality-tv experience of the job market. When candidates see employees enjoying work, having fulfilling and purposeful experiences, or simply enjoying the best aspects of work, this drives the employer's brand across to attract candidates.

Secondly, referrals from existing employees can be another valuable talent attraction tool. Employers provide incentives for existing employees to make referrals. The result can boost morale for the employees, according to Barretto, and it definitely is a boost to their paychecks when referrals are rewarded with finances, gift cards, or extra employee discounts. Another unintended consequence is deeper buy-in to the cultural experience from the referring team member. They are most likely to further demonstrate the desired culture and are also likely to try to positively influence the cultural experience of the candidates they refer.

Thirdly, companies that are accommodating to their employees are highly attractive. When their employees are seen getting recognition and rewards, working from home offices, enjoying fun activities and perks, taking fun work trips, bringing pets to work, playing breakroom games, etc., this becomes a draw for candidates who desire that experience. Based on an SHRM article by Katie Burke, called "Shaping a Culture for Talent Attraction," Burke agrees with Barretto in her advice to "listen to what people want versus the reality that's easiest for you" and "the future is flexible" (Burke, 2022). Burke elaborates to share the data from a Work From Home Research Project that now challenges employers to rethink their stance on work-from-home and its impact on the productivity level. She makes the case for flexibility as it relates to talent attraction as well as retention. Burke further emphasizes the benefit of listening to employees when it comes to flexibility. Sometimes (not always) what employees want *is* doable, if employers listen and get creative, what employers learn can lead to a competitive edge and greater recruitment attraction (Burke, 2022)

Have you ever read a job description that sounded more like a beautiful story of mission and purpose than a list of duties and responsibilities? This brings us to Barretto's fourth strategy. Companies are taking advantage of the job description and posting space to really paint a picture of, not only the company's culture but the company's central purpose for being. These postings are now giving a window into what it's like being in the role – what makes the position fulfilling. This new approach captures the 'why' before it gets into the 'what' and 'how' of the role. As Simon Sinek popularized, connecting people with your 'why' is much more important. If you capture the candidate on 'why,' then you have met the *new* priority objective of job postings and descriptions and gained a one-up on most of the competition who focus on glorifying everything they are, versus what they believe.

For the fifth recommendation, making connections through social media recruiting, per Barretto, is a key to attraction. For this strategy, I think we are all aware of the phobia people are developing against *salesy* in-mail approaches. However, back to the basics of truly building relationships, companies and individuals who know how to make a real and deeper relationship with people through social media are at a much greater advantage. People love to buy but do not want to be sold. The key to great social media usage for recruitment is creating information in formats and using vehicles that are interesting and attractive to those who need to be attracted to it. Relationships cost fewer dollars but require more time, appreciative attention, and sincerity. This is why larger organizations must be strategic. Smaller companies still have the ability, oftentimes, to make a more personal connection and to give a more individualized experience.

So, becoming attractive and magnetic is very doable, with intention and strategic action. However, more critically, companies must understand the importance of not only attracting but attracting what they *need*. Attractive companies naturally attract the kind of demographic that fits what they already are. Attracting strategically and inclusively, requires another level of planning and intention.

It first requires an honest look at what the organization has, as well as being open to having something different. This self-evaluation and benchmarking can be done against statistical demographics in the labor pool or region. For example, specifically who is in the population or talent pool for the role, and are our hires in proportion to that ratio or breakdown? Companies can measure against specific diversity goals. Has the company set specific goals of representation that they would like to reach? What about measuring against the expectations of stakeholders or even the ideal consumer group? What do the employees expect and view as diverse? What about consumers who use the product or patronize the business – is the company meeting their expectations?

Recognize what is hindering the diversity for the roles or what is working in opposition, such as bias. Do you know what biases truly are?

I will never forget listening to a hiring manager, as he shared with a diverse group of high school students about how quickly he hired a student who made great conversation during his interview. What was this great conversation, you may ask. The student sat in front of his wallmounted buck head during his Zoom interview, which spurred a conversation about hunting, and that happened to be the interviewer's favorite sport. 'He was hired immediately!' he bragged - no interview necessary. This is called 'assimilation' or 'similar-to-me' bias, which basically means the more the candidate has in common with the interviewer, the higher the likelihood of hiring, even when the traits don't relate to the job, such as going to the same school, growing up in the same neighborhood, enjoying the same hobbies, etc. This seems innocent, but this has unintended consequences. What happens? people end up with a team that is just like *them*. The process has the impact of repelling or disqualifying those who may, in contrast, prefer basketball, swimming, dancing or even soccer as a favorite hobby. Maybe they grew up on the other side of the tracks or even in a different country and have absolutely nothing in common with the interviewer. Where does this leave those candidates?

Teams must evaluate the biases that are at work. Stereotyping is judging someone based on their group, rather than their individual characteristics. Maybe a man *can* be a good candidate for a receptionist or administrative assistant role, and a woman can be the perfect fit for a high-travel technology role. How do we reprogram our minds to somehow offset our unconscious thoughts? How do we undo the wrongs that are committed in our subconscious brains? The interviewer and interviewee both go in with curiosity and a determination to be interested in others – not only in what we have in common but in our differences.

This is a fine line since we want to maintain professionalism during an interview or even during those initial conversations leading to interviews. However, showing genuine interest in others may be as simple as saying, 'I'm intrigued... Tell me more about that, or what did you enjoy most about that...' Then, follow that with sincere regard or admiration of the uniqueness. This goes both ways – job seeker and company. Both can and should show a genuine interest in understanding and learning about what makes the other unique and/or different. What is the value-add to giving this intentional focus and attention to differences? Everyone tends to enjoy being appreciated, and finding appreciation is both inclusive and attractive.

There are other very easy ways to equalize the hiring process. Conduct structured interviews – asking similar questions during all interviews for the same position gives a better method of rating people on the same criteria. Keep the standards – if the standards are lowered or raised for any one candidate, change the standards for all – and if needed, change the prerequisites for the role altogether to ensure equity across the organization. Involve a larger, representative group in the interview process, and this panel is not limited to leaders. Peers may also make good panelists, with interview training, because they may bring diversity and more in-depth knowledge of the day-to-day duties of the role. Most importantly, regularly and consistently educate interviewers regarding interview errors and how to conduct effective interviews. Most exclusion happens, because managers and interviewers are trying to relate to candidates, attempting to be conversational, and are not aware they are unintentionally setting up roadblocks to inclusion.

Do employers set out to be exclusive? Most likely, no. The sourcing of candidates, posting of roles, and engagement through branding and employee life promotions are intended to be attractive – not exclusive. Most employers and individuals believe they are inclusive, but everyone has hidden patterns of exclusion. Realizing where the patterns lie and uncovering and replacing them with more effective practices, gives companies a competitive advantage. When employers begin to ask basic questions, the truth is uncovered:

- How can the company be more inclusive?
- Who are the brand ambassadors, and are they representative of what/who the company wants to attract? Recruiters? Employee spotlights? News/media articles?
- What shows up on the company's profiles? Social media, leadership team, website? Search engines?

Realizing where there are patterns of exclusion, companies can then begin to focus on a more inclusive strategy to *show up* publicly as a representation of what is desired.

Anyone who has developed a marketing strategy has encountered the 'avatar.' The avatar is the fictitious representation of the 'person' the marketer wants to attract. For example, these avatars are given names and descriptors – entire personas are built around them – in order to develop the full strategy for attracting that 'type.' I do not suggest building avatars, but I do suggest thinking about the full spectrum of people the employer should legally and holistically be trying to bring. Figure out how to attract all of them – that simple. Expand the reach of the brand. For example, while LinkedIn is a great resource for recruitment, engaging TikTok, Instagram, Facebook reels, YouTube shorts, and other avenues expands the employer's reach to an entirely different segment.

Consider engaging existing team members of representative populations to pitch ideas, and do not narrow diversity only to basic differences – yes, think about race, but think much more broadly than that. Differences are innumerable, and the marketing strategies for candidates can and should be refreshed and improved continuously, while aligning back to the company's goals, values, and vision.

As organizations develop their brand, create perks and benefits, and connect with people on social media, expanding attraction is realizing that the focus needs to be broader, and this broadened attraction does not happen by accident – it is intentional.

Not only does the employer 'talent magnet' need to be strong enough, but it also needs to attract what the company *needs* – not just what it already has. What are companies doing well, and what needs to change?

CHAPTER 3

If you're happy, please tell that to your face.

If HR is the heart of the organization, front-line leaders and managers are the *face*. Not only do employees encounter direct leaders and front-line workers on a daily basis, but front-line and middle managers are often the first internal department representatives involved in the interviewing process.

Just before authoring this ebook, after 19 years of gainful employment, I am completely surprised by the level at which leaders engaged during the job match process. Many of my colleagues commented on the shocking difference between who some organization claim they are (the mission and overall branded values) versus what the jobseeker experienced.

There are various fresh instances of leaders being a less-than-stellar reflection of the company's values. For example, on a third interview, one colleague was interviewed by a panel, including meeting the hiring manager for the first time. In that interview and the next, the hiring manager is clearly unengaged both times, does not ask questions, and basically continues working during the entire video interview. On another occasion, a male hiring manager repeatedly questions the female candidate about why she is interested in the role and explains how difficult the role is going to be, spending much more time talking than listening during the interview.

For yet another example, a hiring manager decides the individual is not the right 'fit' for the role but cannot explain what that means. Finally, a hiring manager, having already drawn a conclusion prior to the interview, keeps a candidate waiting for an extended period of time, begins the interview quite late, then abbreviates the interview and quickly dismisses the candidate.

While these examples may be more extreme occurrences, they are not uncommon. When a manager leads an interview rigidly or impersonally, asks illegal questions, or makes inappropriate comments, all of the marketing and branding strategies and even HR's attempt at an excellent candidate experience is often voided. While HR and branding should ensure not to oversell the employee experience, leaders should be careful not to undermine the culture, either.

When leaders are not brand ambassadors, does the company have the ability to attract and retain talent? Find and remediate leaders who impede culture and repel talent. When the 'Employee Experience,' isn't the *employees' experience* companies struggle to become and remain a place where people want to work.

Is it good enough to master the overall employee experience brand, to check all of the boxes for attractive companies? In *Nine Lies About Work*, Marcus Buckingham and Ashley Goodall challenge us to rethink what employees want. 'More than people care about which company they work for, they care which team they're on. (Buckingham & Goodall, 2019).' Leaders are the faces of our teams. Do leaders live the core values, embrace the brand, create the right employee and candidate experience, and reflect the heart of the organization? If our *HeaRt* is smiling, our face should follow suit. *We're never fully dressed without a smile.* Front-line leaders, support services, administrative support, and anyone who engages with candidates, applicants, and team members as a conduit or process manager on a daily basis, should reflect the culture, values, and heart of the organization.

CHAPTER 4

See beyond the resume.

There are many screening methods that drastically decrease the talent pool and exclude what may be 'diamonds in the rough,' which is the phrase coined by the unassuming appearance of a rough diamond before it is uncovered and cut. Would we prefer to have a rough diamond or a perfectly formed piece of glass? This analogy reflects a few key points. Not every exquisitely formatted and worded resume is reflective of an equally outstanding candidate. On the other side of that analogy, a simpler, less extravagant, and extensive resume may not imply a lesser candidate.

Having reviewed over thirty thousand (30,000) resumes in my career, I strongly recommend well-formatted resumes. What does a well-done resume say about a candidate? A well-formatted resume reflects the care and consideration given to the formatting process. However, what happens if a reviewer pre-judges a resume that is not pristinely formatted or written with as much detail? A person who has rarely or never been unemployed may not have a well-polished resume. Maybe five, ten, or more years have passed since the job seeker needed a resume. To have a resume professionally created, a candidate could spend around five hundred ($500). Is it fair that a less qualified candidate could spend five hundred dollars to have a resume professionally done, and in some cases *padded*, while another more qualified candidate may dust off and tweak an old resume for the first time in years?

The same week in which I am writing this, I interviewed a candidate with a very well-written resume, but during this interview, there is apparently a very stark difference between what the candidate said in the behavioral interview and what is on the resume. In fact, when asked about a very specific experience, the candidate says, 'I've never done that before,' while *that* was written expressly on their resume in their job duties for a previous role. Clearly, a resume's format cannot and should not be the only factor for first-level screening. Now, this does not imply that a resume sprinkled with misspellings and errors is acceptable - it is not.

There are numerous free tools for good resumes. For example, a job seeker may use Microsoft Word to pull a resume template from which to work. Additionally, searching free resources such as previous job descriptions or online resources such as job postings or the O*net Online jobs and statistical database (onetonline.org) is a great starting point for duties, knowledge, skills, and abilities for specific roles. LinkedIn has a wonderful resume builder that assists with identifying free key terms that should be used in the resume, based on the job for which the resume is being used. These resources level the playing field for those who need cost-effective resources for resume building.

Name discrimination is still a thing. Screening out by name or the name's appeal or ease of pronunciation is definitely not a valid screening process. However, based on preconceived notions. stereotypes, and certainly unconscious bias, reviewers often show adverse responses to certain names. Take a moment to search online for a list of ethnic names (even by race or country) and become aware of how your mind and emotions automatically respond to certain names, what assumptions are made about the person holding the name (how they may look, talk, or behave), and whether you can pronounce the name with ease. Those factors can create an unintended adverse treatment for those name holders. As an example, recently I assisted a multitude of highly skilled and qualified team members with job placement. I begin to see many of them obtain employment, one by one. I am super excited to see the progress, but I am as disappointed to see who is left behind. Equally as qualified, with resumes as well done, and surely applying for high-needs roles, most of those remaining unemployed have ethnic-type names. The name could and would, at first reading, be associated with a minority.

In my experience, I see firsthand how a person's name easily becomes the talk of the office or the central focus of an inappropriate joke. When the reality settles in, the applicant may miss out on an opportunity simply because of a birth name.

Approximately one year ago (in 2021), a group of researchers from the University of California School of Law (Bault Hall - Aug 2022) conducted a study of over eighty-three thousand (83,000) fictitious applications with randomized characteristics sent to one hundred and eight (108) of the largest US companies. Keep in mind these are large, fortune 500 companies. Their findings reveal that the probability of a callback was decreased by 9% for distinctively 'black names' within the first thirty (30) days. Another study by a group of economists in higher education revealed an eight percent (8%) gap in job placement rates for candidates with hard-to-pronounce names. In a meta-analysis by Quillian et al. (2017), nonminority applicants typically received a callback rate 36% higher than 'black' applicants in the US correspondence experiments (Kline et al., 2021). The larger firms tend to perform better, but smaller organizations have disproportionately more severe discrimination, which is not surprising. Realistically, I do not get too caught up in the statistics, realizing that relationships and getting to know people matter. However, what happens when a person never gets that opportunity to be *known* beyond the 'name' on the application? Whether reviewing the research-based studies or simply experiencing the realities firsthand, we can optimistically assume that most reviewers likely have no ill intent but are victims of their own skew in discretionary judgment. To combat name discrimination, some companies are doing blind resumes – no name, address, or identifiable information is provided to anyone until absolutely necessary. What do you think of that? I think, 'let's move on to the next, less controversial point.'

Resumes often show schools, hometowns, and other details that reviewers may see as more or less impressive. Is this a fair assessment? Is this still a factor? As for schools (post-secondary, etc), going to a prestigious university can be good – great even. However, depending on the course of study and even the individual circumstances, a less-impressive school takes nothing away from a diligent person's potential or achievements. Factors that may impact school choice are widely varied, for example, financial capacity, personal or family responsibilities, cost-saving factors, family makeup, convenience, or a number of others. Someone attending a smaller college or university may spend more focused time with professors, take more care with projects and research, and be more active on campus, building more solid social and leadership skills, for example. While a person attending a reputable university may not have performed well or truly embraced the rigor of effective learning. I had the pleasure of smaller classrooms at Texarkana Community College and Texas A&M University - Texarkana. Yet, I spent no less time and rigor on my assignments, because I valued the experience and feel strongly about supporting local colleges and also a more affordable education. Finally, in terms of hometown advantage (where a person was born or grew up), coming from a town of two thousand has no known implication on I.Q. Maya Angelou, Former President Bill Clinton, Ellen DeGeneres, and Oprah Winfrey all came from towns of less than ten thousand (10,000 in population), to name a few. Great things can come from small places.

Former job titles and years of experience deserve a closer look. Not all job descriptions and titles are universally used. Often a job title may be different, but the core duties and responsibilities are the same. Another common occurrence is people wearing multiple hats for smaller organizations. Therefore, the actual duties are much broader than the description. When evaluating roles, both from the job seeker and the employer standpoint, think of ways to use interchangeable titles, search for specific duties and competencies, and apply human intelligence to the search – not simply rely on machine learning or artificial intelligence processes. As the world changes, jobs have changed at a rapid pace, meaning job descriptions are changing much more rapidly. If tenure is to remain a determining factor for roles, the gap between required experience and that of job seekers will continue to broaden. Tenure is relative. Both parties must consider the quality of experiences and understand that the quality of the experience is not necessarily based on tenure. The quality of work experience is based on how engaged the person is in these experiences. Ten years with a prestigious company where performance standards are low is likely less valuable than a one-year internship with intentional, hands-on learning experiences. Would an employer prefer to have someone who has done the same job duties, using essentially the same methods for ten years or a less tenured person who is agile, ready to adapt, and open to finding the most efficient and effective ways to work?

Companies are becoming more innovative with the application review process, and this indicates a preparedness to face the realities of the future workforce, which quite probably has fewer people available to accomplish the mission.

Employers who are willing to reimagine (not lower) standards, are looking for better ways to get things done. They are a place where team members feel valued and a part of a greater mission - able to help solve the problems of the future.

CHAPTER 5

Place less weight on years; more weight on 'blood, sweat and tears.'

Blood, sweat and tears, also known as *sweat equity* is just that - the value gained from investing painstaking effort and *grit*. So, if employers are not looking *quite* as heavily at tenure and years of experience as the main factor to predict success, what becomes the focus of their pursuits? If we are looking for a true predictor of success, we cannot assume that past performance will guarantee future success, although past performance *is* a good indication. Additionally, *Nine Lies About Work* inspires us to look at forward-thinking predictors of success: momentum, agility/adaptability, social/emotional intelligence, self-awareness, ability to gain trust, and listening skills. Momentum describes how much energy the person puts into doing their work. Agility and adaptability tell us this person can bounce back, learn from errors, and redirect easily when the objectives shift or change and they experience unexpected interruptions. When workloads change or difficult problems arise, agility and adaptability are key. The right kind of employee does not need the perfect scenario to accomplish the mission – they know how to prevail.

When evaluating our own strengths and weaknesses, preparing for job interviews or interviewing others, how do we demonstrate or measure these practical success factors? Behavioral questions are the highest form of interview questions. They challenge the candidate to demonstrate real-life experiences, not just chirp back what they 'will' do in the role if hired. Using this standard format, let's look at a few examples that demonstrate success factors, as defined by Buchkingham and Goodman.

- **Have you had to deal with a complex problem, and how did you solve it:** My team members usually come to me for ideas on how to solve complex problems, for example, a deadline was moved up, and we had to reevaluate our projects and team capacity to find a way to finish on time, while managing other projects, and I... We worked as a team to solve the problem together and were able to meet our deadline. (an example that somewhat resembles the role demonstrates what the person *did*). This indicates collaboration and the ability to develop trust, and the team members' agility (adapting to change quickly).

- **How do you manage?** I lead with sincerity, try to create a safe place for my team, give clear direction, and never ask them to do anything I wouldn't do. For example, during team meetings, when team members realized someone made an error I noticed there was blaming and a lack of ownership. As the leader, I realized that I needed to set an example of how to respond to my mistakes and reassure the team that mistakes are not failures, but learning opportunities. I began sharing my errors and how I solved them, even asking for the team members' input and feedback. When others made mistakes, I addressed them peacefully and used the opportunity to help the individual during one-on-

one time. Now, the team is not ashamed to admit errors, and is able to make quicker improvements. (Demonstrates self-awareness, social/emotional intelligence)

Both employers and job seekers must begin to value the traits that will be most impactful to the organization long term. It is okay to be high on total tenure or work experience (even as an organization), but not at the risk of being low on true success factors, which are a better predictor of success than past performance.

CHAPTER 6

Let them wear their CROWN.

Crown stands for Creating a Respectful and Open World for Natural Hair, and the so-named act, the Crown Act, has been introduced in over twenty-nine (29) states and even at the federal level. So, when it comes to the hiring process, handbooks, dress codes, and even what is defined as 'professional image,' companies are rethinking, and job seekers are becoming less uncomfortable with the natural look.

As a woman with kinky hair, for many years I have felt discomfort with wearing my natural hair to work – not because of my personal concerns, though it *is* quite unruly, but because of how I might be perceived. Naturally, kinky hair can be extremely tough to manage into more mainstream styles, while naturally, kinky hair *loves* cornrows, braids, twists, locs, etc. However, I wonder 'if will I be seen as professional. Will everyone embrace this version of me?'

These concerns become less burdensome when a person is higher in rank and authority. However, for an entry- to a mid-career level team member, seeking approval and opportunities, this is a real challenge. I will never forget the day I told a young lady, about fifteen years ago, that her hairstyle would likely be a hindrance for her hiring manager interview. This young lady was ahead of her time, while I was living in a time warp. My role could and should have been as an advocate, but I had no backing, or courage.

Realistically, the large locs, piled upon the top of her crown in a giant bun would not have passed the 'professional image' test in that banking environment. But, was that fair to her? No.

The Crown Act is making waves across the country, and I predict that it will be the next big change to protected classes. We must soon adapt to cultural and ethnic influences on image and understand how professionalism is defined across cultures.

Even now, there are some states in which the natural crown is protected from discrimination already.

When evaluating candidates for roles, *gone are the days* when professional headshots were simply omitted from resumes, in an effort to protect identities and avoid discrimination. LinkedIn has literally *blown everyone's cover*, as it is the largest repository of resumes and professional headshots in the world. Even without LinkedIn, some individuals have gotten very vocal about how they scout social media to see what their candidates are up to. As a trained HR professional, I see all kinds of problems with snooping on social media pages that are not meant for professional use – namely access to protected information ranging from the latest trip to the ER, to family structure, sexual orientation, and more – just by scrolling on a publicly available non-professional profile. I strongly warn managers and recruiters against crossing those boundaries.

However, with accessibility on LinkedIn, who has to? Now, candidates will have their locs, braids, and natural crowns exposed. Even if the professional headshot has the silk-wrapped or cleanly faded version of the applicant, what happens in the heat of the summer when the applicant walks in with naturally frizzy locs in a top-knot or braids down the back, with a hint of color? Is that a mark against professional image?

How many managers make the case regarding the impact of 'professional image' (such as hair) on positions that require public, consumer, or social interaction? Realistically, studies have shown heightened crown discrimination in positions that are consumer or public-facing. Do companies consider the reverse impact of excluding diverse hair? Consumers have diverse hair. Consumers and the public are engaging with the teams. What is the positive impact of consumers seeing a person across the desk or across the counter who has hair like them?

There are at least a few subliminal messages that come from an openness to hiring candidates with natural crowns. 1) We accept you, 2) You belong, 3) We want your business, and 4) We value you as a unique individual (whether employee or customer).

What defines a 'normal' image anymore anyway? Culturally, as a world full of travel and relocation, we have every opportunity to embrace such a great variety of norms, that we must be careful about what we call 'normal' and 'professional,' namely as it relates to the parts of individuals that are innate and unchangeable. One cannot change the natural texture or unruliness of the hair. While it can be managed and tamed, there are limits and certainly more conducive options.

The Crown Act may be a gateway to other forms of expression with the hair, such as wearing natural gray, openness to a wider variety of hair coloring, and of course, the bearded male image that has taken the world of work by surprise.

As companies begin to review handbooks and dress

codes, they should consider finding ways to gain representative feedback for revisions, be on the lookout for new legislation, and prepare to embrace the new world of natural hair.

CHAPTER 7

True attraction is not robotic, but human.

A.I. is not human – it is artificial intelligence, by name and indeed. A.I. is based on statistical data, human-empowered machine learning processes, and usually strenuous testing of whatever data is input. Should and can A.I. fully replace the human element of applicant screening?

Many employers are adapting resume screening tools that remove the human element from the screening process. This is especially true for very large organizations.

A colleague learned that another was in the market for a new job in the same industry as him - HR. The applicant explained that he had applied for multiple roles at the colleague's large organization, many of which he was at the very least, qualified to apply for – met the requirements as well as preferences. Within less than twelve hours, his applications were rejected each time, stating 'we are moving forward with other, better-qualified candidates.' The colleague disclosed that she had experienced the same issue and received a job interview based on a referral from someone internally. Of course, he then tried sending his resume through the colleague in hopes of a better response and received a call. However, after learning that bit of knowledge, he was discouraged and disappointed in the organization's noninclusive processes, not sure if that organization was the place for him. Having to know someone in order to receive consideration – was definitely not an accurate reflection of their extensive website and massive branding strategy. He was clearly a competitive candidate. Why wasn't the A.I. working?

Using A.I. for screening might implicate inaccurate or unreliable sifting.for quality assurance, and to avoid missing valuable candidates, the human element of validation is necessary during the resume screening process. Trust, but verify. Trust the A.I., but validate that it is working correctly.

Is this simply another thing for people to complain about? Well, the Equal Employment Opportunity (EEOC) and the U.S. The Department of Justice (DOJ) do not think so. During this summer of 2022, the EEOC announced that some AI employment tools may create disability discrimination. California is among the first states to propose regulating employers' use of algorithms and AI. New York City employers are on pins and needles now – on October 25, 2022, the city enacted legislation requiring a "bias audit" *and* disclosures if they use artificial intelligence (AI) to make certain automated employment-related decisions. This NYC law change is in place from January 1, 2023. Not anything really new, but Illinois has taken the reins and required employers to disclose the use of AI analysis for artificial intelligence video interviews, and this went into effect at the beginning of 2020.

What, then, becomes the role of A.I. in the screening process to ensure a more inclusive process? Though A.I. is a great timesaver, perhaps employers who attract talent understand the importance of laying eyes on more resumes, even if that means taking more time or validating the A.I. results by auditing excluded resumes.

Diamond mining has been around for thousands of

years, and yet only some of the mining plants are fully automated. Imagine how many diamonds might be missed without adequate quality control.

Yet, for the sake of time, reviewers often do not give excluded resumes a second look. A key factor in ensuring the highest quality review process is measuring input demographics ratios versus output ratios. What is the percentage of female applicants going into the system, versus the percentage of female applicants remaining after sifting, for example? Repeating that process with a variety of key categories can ensure that the A.I. is working.

You may wonder 'what is the purpose of disclosing the use of A.I. to candidates during the applicant process?' Maybe seeing that notice may prompt an applicant to revisit their resume, ensuring that their resume can, in fact, pass the A.I. test.

What are some of the key factors to enhance the resume and better ensure success through the automated system? With all of the tools available, tailoring a resume to a specific job or type of role is a necessary step if a jobseeker wants to be competitive. Based on the role, there are keywords that probably should be included in real job duties and responsibilities. The key to this step is strategically documenting past and current work experience. Know or find the key words for the role (maybe even in the job posting), and ensure that the resume is not missing words and duties that the system *wants*. A.I. is not the human eye. It is using search tools. This is why a plainly formatted document is likely going to scan into the system much better than one with a lot of graphics. Choose common, universal fonts. Focus more on words than pictures or charts. The A.I. engine is mainly parsing the resume for the right words.

The way resumes are screened has changed quite a bit with A.I., but the way job seekers and employers find one another has not changed as much as we might think. The key to inclusive connection is *effort*. How much initiative will the job seeker and employer take to ensure an equitable process? The most successful employers are reviewing resumes with intentional inclusion. In a world where job seekers have more options, job seekers are most interested in employers who actually keep the *human* in the talent attraction process.

CONCLUSION

Are we truly ready to make the shift from talent acquisition to talent attraction? Getting ahead will set a new pace, take advantage of a new era in changing people processes, and place employers and job seekers at the top of the ranks. Here are some of the key areas we have uncovered:

Talent is not acquired, but borrowed. Now, we fundamentally focus on making a heart connection between employers and job seekers, rather than trying to compete only with the traditional aspects of an employee package. In this way, employers and job seekers look for a true win-win opportunity and discover that the gateway to high performance and fulfillment in any role is igniting the passion behind what we are achieving.

Yet, inclusive attraction is more than just becoming that magnet for talent. To be inclusive, employers are transitioning from attracting only what they already *are* to attracting what they need. The intentionality behind inclusive attraction ensures that there is a strong pull, not just for talent, but for the right talent.

In chapter three, we addressed the opportunities many organizations have to capture candidates through a strong front-line and mid-level leadership culture. If leaders and those most visible to teams and candidates do not reflect or embrace the culture, or have strong biases, the companies have wasted the financial investment on inclusive candidate marketing and branding. Over the last few years of focus in other areas, adequate training and refresher training for leaders is something that many organizations have allowed to digress. A company's accurate measurement of inclusivity is how inclusive the front-line and direct leaders are.

Fourthly, seeing beyond the resume opens our eyes to the possibilities. Many items on the resume, including layout, length, names, job titles, schools and hometowns can be misleading if the reviewer is not trained to counteract and balance assumptions that *may* be incorrect. Talent and skills shortages are requiring us to look a little deeper.

As we venture to focus more on candidate quality, we place less weight on years of service and more weight on the true predictors of success.

Maybe it seemed like a sidebar chapter, but for so many, the CROWN Acts represent a sigh of relief – finally having backing to support a person's ability to embrace the natural methods of hair maintenance and protective styling. Chapter six is dedicated to our understanding of this legislation as well as its impact on inclusivity and belonging.

Finally, as with relationships, true attraction is not robotic. The human element remains a vital part of the process, but as we move ahead, we cannot deny the pressures and demands compounding on our time and resources. Artificial Intelligence (A.I.), being a time saver, may be here to stay, and that means both employers and job seekers must adapt. Those who adapt will lead in a new dispensation of technological efficiencies, while realizing that the greatest, most complex machine ever invented is the human.

God made something that can never be replaced, which comes in approximately eight billion varieties, is full of talent, is motivated by what it loves, and can never truly be acquired – a human being is an invaluable resource that must be attracted.

ABOUT THE AUTHOR

LaTonya Darneish McElroy SPHR, SHRM-SCP/TA has been in the field of Human Resources for nearly two decades, and her first role was in Staffing (Talent Attraction). Seeing the metamorphosis of the role of employers, LaTonya is passionate about creating healthy partnerships between people and organizations, as the foundation for personal and corporate growth that is sustainable. In this book, LaTonya inspires employers and job seekers to discover the value of attraction.

As a Growth Enthusiast, she believes in growing everything, including people, mindsets, careers, processes, teams, companies, finances, and even gardens – yes, all kinds of gardens. Her specialty is identifying what is needed and cultivating for continuous development.

LaTonya serves as a full-time Consultant and Advisor, speaking via training, live experiences, and providing various forms of business and personal consultation. LaTonya's goal is being a positive influence for professionals, HR teams, businesses, families and our communities. As a person of faith, everything she does has a faith foundation, which LaTonya sees as a success factor.

Membership Affiliations:

Society for Human Resources Management (SHRM)

Texas State SHRM Council - District Director NE Texas

LATONYA MCELROY

Tri-State SHRM Chapter Officer

Jack & Jill of America, Inc.

Greater Texarkana Chamber of Commerce

Education, Hospital & Other Local Nonprofit Board Volunteer

Local Christian Church Leader and Volunteer

WORKS CITED:

Barretto, Wileen. "5 Innovative Talent Attraction Strategies." Jobsoid.com, Wileen Barretto, 24 June 2021, https://www.jobsoid.com/5-innovative-talent-attraction-strategies/.

Buckingham, M., & Goodall, A. (2019). Nine Lies About Work: A Freethinking Leader's Guide to the Real World. Harvard Business Review Press.

Burke, K. (2022). https://www.shrm.org/executive/resources/people-strategy-journal/spring2022/pages/feature-culture-talent-attraction-burke.aspx. SHRM Executive Network. shrm.org

Kline, P., Rose, E. K., & Walters, C. R. (2021). SYSTEMIC DISCRIMINATION AMONG LARGE U.S. EMPLOYERS. University of California, Berkeley. https://eml.berkeley.edu//~crwalters/papers/randres.pdf

www.ingramcontent.com/pod-product-compliance
Lightning Source LLC
Chambersburg PA
CBHW050315220526
45465CB00005B/1998